BABE RUTH

by
William R. Sanford
&
Carl R. Green

New York

Maxwell Macmillan Canada
Toronto

Maxwell Macmillan International
New York Oxford Singapore Sydney

Library of Congress Cataloging-in-Publication Data
Sanford, William R. (William Reynolds)
    Babe Ruth / by William R. Sanford and Carl R. Green. — 1st ed.
      p. cm. — (Sports immortals)
    Includes bibliographical references and index.
    Summary: The life story of the greatest home-run hitter, Babe Ruth, baseball player extraordinaire.
    ISBN 0-89686-741-2
    1. Ruth, Babe, 1895–1948—Juvenile literature. 2. Baseball players—United States—Biography—Juvenile literature. [1.
Ruth, Babe, 1895–1948. 2. Baseball players.] I. Green, Carl R. II. Title. III. Series.
GV865.R8S26   1992
796.357'092—dc20
[B]   91-21639

Photo Credits
Cover: National Baseball Library, Cooperstown, NY
National Baseball Library, Cooperstown, NY: 4, 11, 12, 15, 17, 19, 22, 24, 26, 28, 31, 33, 37, 38, 41, 42
AP—Wide World Photos: 7, 8, 21, 34

CRESTWOOD HOUSE

Macmillan Publishing Company
866 Third Avenue
New York, NY 10022

Maxwell Macmillan Canada, Inc.
1200 Eglinton Avenue East
Suite 200
Don Mills, Ontario M3C 3N1

Macmillan Publishing Company is part of the Maxwell Communication Group of Companies.

Produced by Flying Fish Studio

Printed in the United States of America

First edition

10 9 8 7 6 5 4 3 2 1

CONTENTS

The Babe Calls His Shot 5

A Street Kid Grows Up 9

The Babe's Short Road to the Majors....................11

The Red Sox Years 15

The Babe Becomes a Yankee 19

The House That Ruth Built................................24

Murderers' Row 28

The Poor Boy Makes Good 30

The End of a Great Career................................35

The Babe's Last Years 38

Babe Ruth, Baseball Immortal 41

Glossary 44

More Good Reading about Babe Ruth 46

Babe Ruth Trivia Quiz....................................47

Index 48

Lou Gehrig (left) *and Babe Ruth*

THE BABE CALLS HIS SHOT

In 1990 *Life* magazine published a list of the century's most important Americans. Only two baseball players made the honor roll. Jackie Robinson was chosen because he broke baseball's color barrier. *Life* called the other, George Herman Ruth, "the greatest baseball player in the history of the game."

George Herman? Baseball knew the New York Yankee slugger better as the Babe. When Babe reached the **major leagues**, teams played for one run at a time. His big bat changed all that. People love home runs, and no one hit them like the Babe.

Some of Babe's 714 homers were game winners. Many came at moments of high drama. But there was one long blast that Babe called his proudest moment in baseball.

The year was 1932. The Yankees were playing the Chicago Cubs in the World Series. Babe was 37, overweight and feeling his age. His legs hurt and he could not always bend down to pick up ground balls. Even so, he had batted .341 and hit 41 home runs that year. The Babe could always swing the bat.

On October 1 the teams met in Chicago for the third game of the Series. The Yankees were leading, two games to none. In the fourth inning, the score was tied, 4–4. Babe Ruth came to the plate with one out and the bases empty. The Cubs shouted insults from their **dugout**. The hometown fans booed.

The Babe lived for moments like that. He watched Charlie Root's first pitch zip past for a strike. Holding up one finger, he yelled, "Strike one!" Root's second pitch was also a strike. Babe held up two fingers. Ahead in the count, Root then wasted two pitches. Babe raised two fingers on his left hand. Then he pointed toward the center-field bleachers with his right hand.

The gesture seemed clear. Babe was going to put the next pitch over the fence. Some say Root's next pitch was a fastball. Others claim it was a change-up curve. Whatever it was, Babe timed it perfectly. The ball exploded off his bat and landed in the distant bleachers.

Later Babe said, "As I hit the ball, every muscle told me I had never hit a better one. I knew that as long as I lived, nothing would ever feel as good as that."

Inspired by the home run, the Yankees went on to win the game and the Series. Then a debate arose. Did the Babe really call his shot? Some claimed the gesture was just a vague wave of his hand. None of the Babe's fans believed that. He was the Sultan of Swat, the Bambino. He was a baseball immortal.

TRIVIA 1* — Hank Aaron broke the Babe's record of 714 lifetime home runs in 1974. How many homers did Aaron belt before he retired?

* Answers to all Trivia Quiz questions can be found on page 47.

*Babe Ruth smacks a double in the first inning of a Yankee/Dodger
exhibition game played in New York.*

The Babe sends the ball over the fence in the fourth inning of a game played in Detroit against the Tigers.

A STREET KID GROWS UP

No one thought young George Ruth would become a rich and famous baseball player. He was a tough street kid who was often in trouble. Looking back, the Babe later summed up his early life. "I was a bum when I was a kid," he said.

The Babe was born in Baltimore, Maryland, on February 6, 1895. George and Kate Ruth never had much luck. Only two of their eight children lived past infancy. They worked hard, but they did not make much money. Big George ran a saloon. Kate helped by tending bar, but she was often ill. With no one to watch him, little George roamed the streets. He almost never went to school.

When little George was seven, his parents gave up on their son. Unable to control him, they sent him to St. Mary's Industrial School. St. Mary's was a **reform school**. The Catholic brothers there took in problem boys and taught them to be useful citizens. Discipline was harsh but fair. The school could not turn George into a gentleman. But it did tame his worst faults.

Little George's first stay at St. Mary's lasted only a month. Two years later he was back. After that he spent eight of the next ten years there. He became a Catholic and served as an altar boy. The brothers taught George to read and write. To prepare him for a job, they trained him to be a tailor. In the tailor shop, he earned six cents a shirt for sewing on collars. Some of the money went for candy, which he shared with the younger boys.

TRIVIA 2

The Babe hit 16 bases-loaded home runs during his career. Who holds the record for bases-loaded homers, and how many did he hit?

Discipline at St. Mary's was in the hands of Brother Matthias. The Boss was a huge man. He stood six feet, six inches tall and weighed 250 pounds. Matthias took a liking to George and became a kind of second father to the boy. For his part, Babe later said, "He was the greatest man I've ever known."

It was Matthias who taught George to play baseball. The big man loved the game. He hit fly balls and grounders to his players by the hour. As Babe put it, "I could hit the first time I picked up a bat. But Brother Matthias made me a fielder."

St. Mary's sponsored over 40 baseball teams. George was a standout hitter and left-handed catcher. He played for the Red Sox, the school's best team. He also played third base and pitched the team's big games. No one at St. Mary's could hit a ball farther than he did. By the time he was 16 he had grown to six feet, two inches and weighed 190 pounds. Despite his size, he was a graceful, natural athlete.

In 1913 the big game was with Mount St. Joseph's College. A large crowd turned out to see George pitch against St. Joe's star. He gave the St. Mary's boys plenty to cheer about. Fourteen St. Joe's batters struck out as St. Mary's won, 6-0. The win was doubly important to George, for he was being watched by a **scout**.

Jack Dunn watched the game from the stands. Dunn owned the Baltimore Orioles, then a **minor league** team. After the game he and George had a long talk. Whatever they said, Dunn came back that winter. With Brother Matthias looking on, he offered George a contract to play for his team. A new world was opening up for the tough street kid.

THE BABE'S SHORT ROAD TO THE MAJORS

George Ruth was 19 when he walked out of St. Mary's in February of 1914. He must have felt like dancing. For starters, he was finally free of the school's strict rules. Best of all, he was going to be a ballplayer. Jack Dunn was paying him $600 to play the game he loved!

Young Babe Ruth

Babe Ruth watches one of his many homers fly over the fence.

By law, George should have stayed at the school until he was 21. Dunn solved that problem too. He became George's legal guardian. The young man said good-bye to his family in early March and boarded a train. He was on his way to **spring training**.

George was the youngest player on the Orioles team. The veterans knew that George was taking his first train ride. When he climbed into his upper berth to sleep, he saw a small net hammock. The older players knew it was meant to hold clothing. They told George he was supposed to rest his pitching arm in the net. The **rookie** did as he was told. He spent a mostly sleepless night with his left arm stuck in the net.

Training camp was a joy for the young man. For the first time in his life, George could eat all the food he wanted. As soon as he finished one huge breakfast, he asked for another. Elevators were also new to him. He spent a happy hour riding up and down, up and down.

The veterans had a good time making fun of George. A team coach heard the teasing and warned that it had to stop. George was one of the owner's babes, he said. Almost at once people began to call him "Babe." From then on the public knew him by that nickname. Many of his teammates called him "Jidge," a slang form of "George." For his part, Babe called most people "Doc" or "Kid." He never could remember names.

TRIVIA 3 Many of the Babe's records have been broken since he retired. What important major league records does he still hold?

On the field, Babe soon showed what he could do. He homered in his first game as an Oriole. On the mound Babe showed equal promise. Pitching against major leaguers, he showed a major league fastball and curve. No one was surprised when the Babe was picked as one of the team's regular players.

Back in Baltimore, sportswriters urged the fans to watch the rookie play. The fans came out—but not to see Babe and the Orioles. They wanted to see the city's new **Federal League** team, the Terrapins. On opening day the Terrapins drew a crowd of 30,000. Only 1,500 paid to see the Orioles. On April 22, fewer than 200 saw Babe pitch a 6–0 **shutout**.

The Babe won games with his arm and with his bat. After a month Dunn raised the Babe's pay to $900. By June the owner was paying his star a veteran's salary of $1,800. Dunn knew that the Terrapins were looking at the Babe. He did not want to lose him.

The Orioles were hot. They won 13 straight and had a firm hold on first place. Sadly, the winning streak did not impress the fans. Crowds of 150 were not enough to pay the bills. By July Dunn was running out of money. The only way he could keep the team going was to sell his stars.

Dunn talked to Philadelphia, but the Athletics said no. He then struck a deal with the Boston Red Sox. The Red Sox agreed to buy the Babe and two other players. The sales price was kept quiet, but the papers said it was about $25,000. The Red Sox had struck it rich in Jack Dunn's fire sale.

THE RED SOX YEARS

Babe Ruth reached Boston on July 12, 1914. Rough Carrigan was the Red Sox manager. He put the Babe into a game that same day. Babe won his first game and lost the second. After that Carrigan kept the rookie on the bench.

The Babe stands on the mound, ready to pitch a fast ball

Sitting on the bench did not change the Babe's style. Proud of his hitting, he took batting practice with the regulars. Some Red Sox veterans found a way to let Babe know he was too pushy. Picking up his bats one day, he found they had been sawed in two.

In August the Red Sox owner sent Babe Ruth back to the minor leagues. His Providence (Rhode Island) Grays needed a left-handed pitcher. The move was a tonic for the Babe. He won his first start, 5–4, helping his own cause with two triples. On top of his game now, he won eight more starts. The Grays won the **pennant**.

When the minor league season ended, the Babe was called back to Boston. Pitching against the Yankees, he won his second game for the Red Sox. Babe also smacked a two-bagger that day. It was his first major league hit.

When the season ended, Babe felt as though he was on top of the world. He had money in his pocket and a steady girl-friend. She was Helen Woodford, a pretty young waitress. The Babe had been courting her ever since he came to Boston. Now, on impulse, he asked Helen to marry him. When she said yes, they ran off to Baltimore to be married. They lived with big George and his new wife that winter. The Babe's mother had been dead for two years.

In March of 1915 young men in Europe were fighting World War I. The Babe worried more about winning baseball games. When the season started, he lost four of his first five games. Then he turned around and won six straight. In the third inning of a game in New York, he hit his first major league home run.

The Red Sox caught fire. The Babe led the way, winning 17 of his last 21 games. The Detroit Tigers made it a close race, but

Babe Ruth pitching a curve ball

the Red Sox held them off. Then they beat the Athletics in the World Series. The Babe's share of the Series money was $3,780. He used part of his check to buy a new bar for his father.

The Red Sox sold Tris Speaker before the start of the 1916 season. Without their best hitter, the team started slowly. Then with the Babe leading the way, the Red Sox began to win. Babe helped nail down the pennant with 23 wins, nine of which were shutouts. In the World Series they beat the Brooklyn Dodgers 2–1 in 14 innings. It was the longest World Series game ever played.

Babe had become a star. In 1917 and 1918 he started 57 games and finished all but four of them. When the United States went to war, he helped sell Liberty bonds. As a married man and a ballplayer, he chose not to enlist in the army.

In his first three years with Boston, Babe hit only nine home runs. In those days, homers were rare. Home Run Baker led the league with eight in 1915. In 1918 the Babe won his first home-run title with 11 homers. The Red Sox played him in the outfield when he was not pitching. That big bat could win ball games.

In 1919 the Babe's salary soared to $10,000. He played every day, pitching only when he was needed. He hit 29 homers that year, breaking a major league record set in 1884. On the mound, he was 9–5. He told the Red Sox he wanted to be paid $20,000 the next year. Otherwise he might not play at all.

TRIVIA 4 Like most ballplayers, the Babe was superstitious. What was most likely to upset him?

An autographed photo of Babe Ruth

THE BABE BECOMES A YANKEE

Money was a big issue as the 1920 season neared. The Babe was spending his as fast as he made it. He loved to party, and he was quick to pay the checks. Because he loved to smoke cigars, he bought an interest in a cigar factory.

Harry Frazee, the new owner of the Red Sox, had troubles of his own. The team was losing money. To make matters worse, the Babe wanted a $10,000 raise. Many of today's stars, of course, make that much a game. In 1920, however, players were at the mercy of their owners. They could not change teams unless they were sold or traded. Most signed for about $3,000.

Frazee turned to the owners of the New York Yankees. Colonel Jacob Ruppert and Colonel Til Huston were his friends. The three men soon worked out a deal. Ruppert and Huston bought the Babe for $100,000 and loaned Frazee another $300,000. The Babe was happy to sign with the Yankees after Ruppert had met his price.

Babe Ruth was now a superstar. When he played, the ballparks were full. Fans loved their hard-hitting, hard-living hero. The Yankee manager, Miller Huggins, did not. He tried—and failed—to put a stop to his outfielder's nightlife. As Babe's roommate Ping Bodie put it, "I don't room with him. I room with his suitcase."

All eyes were on the Babe when the season started. Could he break his record of 29 homers? At first the answer seemed to be no. The Babe was in a **slump**. Then on May 1, 1920, he hit one over the roof of the Polo Grounds. He never looked back. By the end of the 154-game season he had banged out 54 home runs. Only one other player in the league hit more than 44.

Baseball needed the Babe in 1920. That was the year fans

TRIVIA 5

The Babe loved to pull pranks on his teammates. What was his favorite?

Babe Ruth at bat

The Babe with some of his many adoring fans

learned of the Black Sox scandal. Eight Chicago White Sox players had taken money to lose the 1919 World Series. People began to wonder if all the games were fixed. The owners hired Kenesaw Mountain Landis to keep the game honest. Judge Landis did his part by ruling baseball with an iron hand. The Babe's home runs also helped erase thoughts of the scandal.

The owners knew that fans liked to see high-scoring games. They banned trick pitches like the spitball and made the ball more lively. With what was called "rabbit" in the ball, long home runs became more common. For their part, batters copied the Babe's big swing. Strikeouts were no longer a disgrace.

In 1921 the Babe led the Yankees to their first American League pennant. Along with a record 59 homers, he hit .378 and batted in 171 runs. During the season he also pitched and won two games. In one of them he struck out the great Ty Cobb. Playing with a painful elbow, the Babe was held to one homer in the World Series. The Yankees lost to the New York Giants.

The Babe left for a **barnstorming tour** after the season. In doing so, he broke one of Judge Landis's rules. The Judge fined the Babe his share of the World Series money. He also suspended him for the first month of the 1922 season. "We play a game called baseball, not a game called Ruth," the Judge snapped.

The Yankees gave Babe a new $52,000 contract. "I always wanted to make a thousand a week," he said. As for not playing, the Babe was sure the Judge would back down. He went on chasing pretty girls, thick steaks and strong drink. The Babe never worried about the future.

Babe Ruth's awesome hitting helped the Yankees become a record-setting team.

THE HOUSE THAT RUTH BUILT

The year 1922 was a year of bad news and good news for the Yankees. The bad news was that Judge Landis meant what he said: Babe Ruth did not play until May 20. When he did come back, he suffered through a poor year. For the Babe, that meant a drop to 35 home runs and a .315 **batting average**. The good news was that the team won the pennant again.

The Yankees were still playing their home games at the Polo Grounds. As tenants, they paid the Giants $100,000 a year in rent. Now with the Babe drawing big crowds, the Yankees were setting records. In 1920, 1.2 million fans paid to see them play. No other team had ever sold that many tickets.

The Giants were stung by the success of their upstart tenants. In 1920 they told the Yankee owners they would have to move. Ruppert and Huston took up the challenge. They bought land near the Harlem River. Soon workers were putting up a three-deck grandstand with 62,000 seats. The walls were immensely high. Only one fair ball ever cleared those walls. It was hit during an exhibition game by Josh Gibson, a black slugger.

Yankee Stadium opened on April 18, 1923. Crowds jammed the nearby streets and filled the park to bursting. The great march king, John Philip Sousa, led a band concert. Governor Al Smith was there, as was Judge Landis. The Babe had worked hard to get in shape. In his second time at bat, he drilled an outside pitch into the right-field stands. The crowd was thrilled. They had just seen the first home run hit in the new stadium.

Sportswriters began to call the stadium "The House That Ruth Built." After his off year, the Babe was back. His batting average climbed to .393, a lifetime best. In the World Series, the Yankees met the Giants for the third year in a row. This time the Yankees won their first World Series title. The Babe led the way with three home runs, a triple and a double.

In 1924 the Babe won his first and only batting title. He hit .378 and added 46 home runs. Despite his fine year, the Yankees finished two games behind Washington. The team won 18 of its last 22 games, but could not catch the Senators.

The next year was a disaster. The Babe's love of food and drink caught up with him. He collapsed on the way north from spring training. A rumor flashed around the world that he was dead. Rushed to the hospital, he was operated on for an intestinal abscess. Doctors said he had abused his body by eating and drinking too much. With the team stuck in seventh place, the Babe was back in the lineup on June 1.

June 1 was notable for a second reason. On that day Lou Gehrig was put into the game as a **pinch hitter**. Lou took over at first base the next day. He stayed there for a record 2,130 games in a row.

The illness did not change the Babe. After he broke **curfew** once too often, Miller Huggins suspended him. He also fined the Babe $5,000. To make matters worse, the Babe's wife had suffered a nervous breakdown. Helen could no longer cope with the Babe's wild ways. Now cut off from the team, the Babe was in despair. Yankee fans mourned that his great days were over.

TRIVIA 6

How did the Babe beat the heat?

Babe Ruth patiently awaits his turn at bat, carefully planning his hitting.

MURDERERS' ROW

Those who counted Babe Ruth out soon changed their tune. The run-in with Huggins gave the Babe a new outlook. He also listened to New York's future mayor, Jimmy Walker. Walker scolded the Babe for letting down "the dirty-faced kids" who loved him.

Babe Ruth tries to keep his mind mostly on baseball.

Over the next six years Babe kept his mind mostly on baseball. The numbers prove the point. From 1926 through 1931, he averaged 50 home runs a year. There were plenty of singles, doubles and triples as well. He averaged .354 during those years and knocked in 155 runs a year.

In 1927 the Yankees fielded a powerhouse lineup. Some baseball experts call it the greatest team of all time. Pity the poor pitcher who had to face **Murderers' Row**: Babe Ruth (.356), Lou Gehrig (.373), Bob Meusel (.337) and Tony Lazzeri (.309). The Babe went on a home-run binge late in the season. As the last week began he had 56 home runs.

The nation was watching to see if the Babe could break his home-run record of 59. On Tuesday he hit number 57. Numbers 58 and 59 flew out of the park two days later, tying the record. On Friday Babe faced Washington's Tom Zachery. In the eighth inning he drove his sixtieth homer into the right-field seats. After the game he yelled, "Let's see [someone else] match that!"

The record lasted for 34 years. Roger Maris broke it by hitting 61 in 1961. The Babe's fans quickly pointed out that the 1961 season was eight games longer.

The Yankees won the pennant by 19 games in 1927. In the World Series they beat the Pittsburgh Pirates in 4 straight. The Babe hit two more home runs to lead the sweep.

The Babe's home-run record tends to outweigh his other numbers. Between 1914 and 1935 he went to bat 8,396 times and cranked out 2,873 hits. Those hits produced a lifetime batting average of .342. He also scored 2,174 runs and batted in 2,204 more. The Babe was just as proud of his pitching record: 94 wins and only 46 losses. His **earned run average** was a sparkling 2.24.

The numbers alone do not explain the Babe's appeal. Fans loved his style. His Black Betsy bat weighed 52 ounces, far heavier than the bats used by most players. When he swung and missed, his body twisted into a corkscrew. Even his pop flies seemed to take forever to come down. Infielders also had a tough time catching his ground balls. The Babe hit the ball so hard that it tended to take crazy hops.

Pitchers often took the bat out of Babe's hands by walking him. He received 2,056 bases on balls during his career. Yankee fans booed the walks, for they wanted to see the big guy hit the ball. Babe did not like walks either. A pitcher once tried to walk him by throwing a ball 18 inches outside. The Babe simply reached out and pulled the ball into the right-field stands.

Old baseball players still talk about the Babe's swing. No batting coach ever dared try to change it. For all his power, his swing was so smooth, it seemed effortless. But the Babe liked to show the calluses on his hands. "I got those from gripping this old war club," he said. "When I am out after a homer, I try to make mush of this solid ash handle." More often he made mush of the opposing team.

THE POOR BOY MAKES GOOD

Babe Ruth never forgot his childhood. He lived each day as if he were making up for being poor. Although he made a huge salary for his day, he spent it very quickly. His friends often said that he was like a big kid. "I sure like to live as big as I can," he said.

The Babe bought silk shirts by the dozen and wore several outfits a day. He bought a mink coat for Helen and a new car for Brother Matthias. During one World Series party he was told the hotel did not have a piano. Babe bought one and had it delivered to the hotel. Waiters loved his $10 tips. In those days most people were lucky to make $10 for a day's work.

Babe works out on a Florida beach.

Despite his lavish spending, the Babe was a rich man when he left baseball. Christy Walsh and Claire Ruth can take credit for that. Christy was Babe's business manager. Claire was his second wife. The Babe married her after Helen had died in a fire. It was Christy who talked the Babe into saving some of his money. He also set up barnstorming tours, film projects and endorsements. The Babe's name sold everything from autos to underwear. Claire took control of the purse strings. She put her free-spending husband on a budget of $35 a day.

Some of the Babe's projects worked out, others failed. In the days before television, people were hungry to see big league players. Babe's barnstorming team, the Bustin' Babes, drew big crowds wherever they played. Christy made sure the Babe's picture was always in the papers. He even wrote a column that ran with a Babe Ruth by-line.

The Babe liked kids and knew how to talk to them. He once promised to hit a World Series home run for a badly injured boy. True to his word, he went out and hit three against St. Louis. The boy was thrilled—and the newspapers had a great story.

Food was a big part of the Babe's life. He ate huge meals four or five times a day. "Be sure to put lots of lamp chops around the steak," he would tell a waiter. One of his favorite meals was chicken and mashed potatoes. Being the Babe, he ate a whole chicken. A quart of ice cream was the ideal dessert. For a bedtime snack he ate club sandwiches and pigs' knuckles. Then he washed it all down with soda or beer.

The Babe paid a price for eating so much. Before games he drank a glass of bicarbonate of soda to settle his stomach. He called it his "milk." The big meals added weight as well. When he ballooned to 250 pounds his legs looked too thin to support his body. Miller Huggins was always urging him to slim down. The Babe would promise to lose weight and get more rest. He kept his word—until the next time he went out on the town.

For all his high jinks, baseball was the Babe's first love. Along with his clutch hitting, he was a fine fielder and a clever base runner. By 1930 he was making $80,000 a year. At that time it was the highest salary ever paid to a baseball player. Lou Gehrig, a star in his own right, was barely making $10,000.

The news of Babe's big contracts made headlines. As the story goes, someone told him he was making more than President Hoover. "Why not?" the Babe said. "I had a better year than he did."

Young infantile paralysis victims cheer Babe Ruth as the slugger visits New York's Hospital for Joint Diseases.

Babe Ruth's home run hitting changed baseball forever.

THE END OF A GREAT CAREER

Age and injuries slowed the Babe but did not stop him. After setting his home-run record, he played eight more years. In all but the last two he hit over .300. There were days when his bat still smoked. In the 1928 World Series, the Babe cracked out 10 hits in 16 times at bat. Three of the hits were homers.

By 1929 the Yankees were wearing their new pinstripe uniforms. Some said that Colonel Ruppert had ordered the stripes to make the Babe look thinner. That was the year the players wore numbers for the first time. As the number-three hitter, the Babe wore number 3. In July the Babe reached a milestone: home run number 500.

Two months later Miller Huggins died of blood poisoning. The Babe wanted Hug's job, but Colonel Ruppert said no. The feeling was that the Babe could not manage himself. That being so, how could he manage a ball club?

The Great Depression brought hard times in 1930. Out-of-work fans came to the ballpark to forget their troubles. The Babe helped by slugging more crowd-pleasing home runs. In May he hit three in a regular-season game for the first time. Late in the season, he pitched against Boston. The old magic was still there. The Babe went the distance, winning 9–3.

TRIVIA 7

Pitcher Waite Hoyt was the Babe's friend and teammate for 11 seasons. What did the Babe say when Waite left the team after being traded?

Time was working against the Babe. He still wanted to manage, but Ruppert gave the job to Joe McCarthy. When the Babe went to the plate, he had to hit a new, less lively ball. He slammed a home run on opening day, but his legs were hurting. He choked down on the bat and began hitting more singles to left field. Despite the new ball, he hit .373 and blasted home run number 600.

The Babe had his last big year in 1932. The Yankees let him play when he felt like it. Hobbled by aching legs, he often left the game in the late innings. Although his fielding suffered, he still swung the bag well enough to hit .341. Sent to the mound for the last time, he gave up five runs but won the game.

The Yankees met Chicago in the World Series that year. The Cubs yelled that the Babe was old and washed up. The jeers did not upset him. He quieted the bench jockeys with his called-shot home run in game three.

The Babe's big moments were now widely spaced. In 1933 he looked like the Babe of old in the first All-Star Game. Batting in the second inning, he hit the game's first home run. Home run number 700 came in 1934, but the Babe's average fell to .288. That was also the year Ruppert offered him a chance to manage in the minors. An angry Babe refused. A star should not be forced to "try out" as a manager, he said.

 TRIVIA 8 | The Babe is best known as a hitter, but he was also a fine outfielder. How good was his throwing arm?

36

The Babe left the Yankees in the fall of 1934. In 1935 he surprised the baseball world by signing with the Boston Braves. The Braves hoped the Babe's name would sell tickets. His job was to pinch hit, play a little outfield and coach the young players. In the season opener, Babe hit a game-winning home run. After that he struggled to raise his average above .200.

Then came a May game at Pittsburgh. Babe enjoyed one last hurrah. He went four for four, with three home runs. His last major league hit—home run number 714—carried 600 feet.

After that the Babe played in only five more games. His knee hurt and his eyes were playing tricks on him. On June 2, 1935, he quit the team. His career as a ballplayer was over.

George Herman Ruth, one of the most exciting sports figures of modern times

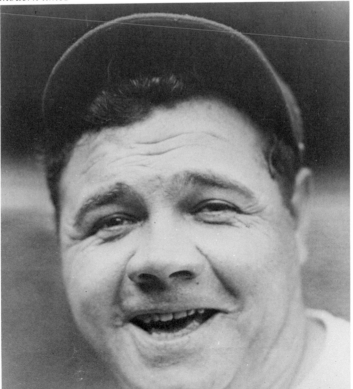

THE BABE'S LAST YEARS

Babe Ruth was only 41 when he left the Braves. He said he had many more years to give to the game he loved. Soon, he hoped, someone would hire him to manage a big league team. The Babe waited, but no offers came. Without baseball to keep him busy, he had time for play and travel. He suited up for a few baseball games with a semipro team. Word that the Babe was playing lured thousands of fans. He also liked to bowl, hunt, fish and play golf. Whatever he played, he played to win.

The crowd watches in amazement as Babe Ruth hits a flying home run during this War Bond Drive at the Polo Grounds in New York.

Claire fussed at the Babe for spending too much time on the golf course. She was happier when she and Babe took a world tour. Foreign countries puzzled him. In Japan he was called "the god of Baseball." In France no one seemed to know who he was.

When they were in New York, the Ruths lived on Riverside Drive. The Babe loved his wife, but he was seldom home. Thanks to Claire, he cut back on his nightlife. Instead of going to parties, the Ruths had friends in to play cards. The Babe also enjoyed the radio. He would leave his pals and hurry home to listen to *Gangbusters*.

The Babe gave baseball one last try in 1938. The Brooklyn Dodgers hired him as a coach. Secretly, Babe thought he was in line for the manager's job. To please the fans, he took batting practice and served as first-base coach. After the games, he talked to the kids and signed their programs.

As a coach, one of the Babe's jobs was to relay signs to base runners. As often as not, he ignored the signs flashed from the bench. That upset the fiery Leo Durocher, the team captain. Leo and the Babe almost had a fight after one game.

The Babe's last hopes died at the end of the season. The club hired Durocher as manager. The Babe retired for the last time and let his weight zoom up to 270 pounds. That brought on two mild heart attacks. In 1942 he lost weight so he could play himself in a film about Lou Gehrig. The strain of acting in *Pride of the Yankees* sent him back to the hospital.

TRIVIA 9 Why did railroad porters hate to see the Babe board their train?

During World War II, the Babe helped raise money to support the war effort. In August 1942 he played in an **old-timers' game** for war relief. Babe hit a high fly that curved foul into the right-field stands. He chose to call it a home run. The crowd stood and cheered as he trotted around the bases.

In 1946 doctors found a cancerous growth in the Babe's neck. By the time he left the hospital he had lost 80 pounds. Somehow he found the strength to visit Mexico City. There, to promote baseball, he hit his final home run.

April 27, 1947, was Babe Ruth Day at Yankee Stadium. The Babe looked gaunt and old as he made his entrance. When he spoke to the hushed crowd, his voice was a raspy croak. He said, "The only real game in the world, I think, is baseball."

The cancer was still growing. In June of 1948 the Babe was too ill to play in a two-inning old-timer's game. Dressed in his old pinstripes, he did manage to shuffle onto the field. Cheers rocked The House That Ruth Built when the crowd saw him. *IN AUG 1948*

Those were the last cheers the Babe heard. Two months later he was dead. As a special tribute, his body lay in state at Yankee Stadium. Tens of thousands of fans filed past the casket to pay their last respects.

TRIVIA 10   Who is the *Baby Ruth* candy bar named for?

Babe Ruth slides safely into home base.

BABE RUTH, BASEBALL IMMORTAL

Was Babe Ruth the greatest baseball player of all time? Among baseball fans that question can always start an argument. Some point out that no one can match the Babe's record as both a pitcher and a hitter. Others give him credit for saving the game after the Black Sox scandal. What is certain is that his home-run hitting changed baseball forever.

One measure of greatness is having a plaque in the National Baseball Hall of Fame. The hall, located at Cooperstown, New York, is a baseball museum. The site is where Abner Doubleday is said to have invented baseball in 1839. Baseball writers pick only a few players for the Hall of Fame each year.

The first players were voted into the Hall of Fame in 1936. The writers made five choices that year. They picked Ty Cobb, Honus Wagner, Christy Mathewson, Walter Johnson—and Babe Ruth. All but Babe were over 50 years old. When he hit a pop fly during the Hall of Fame game, the crowd roared. Fans knew they were watching a living legend.

The Babe treasured his day at the Hall of Fame. He wanted to be remembered. Before he died he wrote a book about his life with the help of Bob Considine. He also set up the Babe Ruth Foundation to help poor kids.

Hollywood rushed to make a movie of his life. It was called *The Babe Ruth Story*. The Ruths wanted a top star to play the part. Instead the role went to a comic, William Bendix. Bendix had to be coached on how to swing a bat. The Babe was taken to see the film shortly before he died. Sadly, he was too ill to enjoy it.

Today it is hard to find the real Babe Ruth. His legend gets in the way. What is certain is that he was a superb athlete. In his prime he played with grace, speed and power. He also had the appetites of a headstrong child. Like a child, he could not admit that his bad habits hurt his career. Too much food and drink shortened his playing days. This lack of self-discipline also kept club owners from hiring him as a manager.

At one time the Babe held 61 major league records. Over the years, many have been smashed. Their loss does not dim his memory. The Babe was larger than life. He was one of the most exciting sports figures of modern times.

Fans paid tribute to the slugger on Babe Ruth Day at Yankee Stadium.

GLOSSARY

barnstorming tour—A tour in which a team travels around the country playing exhibition games during the off-season.

batting average—A measure of a batter's success at the plate. Batting averages are figured by dividing the number of hits by the times at bat. Thus someone who collects 35 hits in 100 at bats would have a batting average of .350.

curfew—The time when ballplayers are supposed to be in bed. Curfews are set and enforced by the team's manager.

dugout—The below-ground shelter in which baseball players sit while they are not playing.

earned run—A run scored by the team at bat without benefit of an error by the defensive team.

earned run average—A measure of a pitcher's success at keeping the opposing team from scoring. Earned run averages are calculated by figuring the number of earned runs allowed per nine innings pitched. Thus a pitcher who allows 9 earned runs in 27 innings would have an earned run average of 3.00.

Federal League—An "outlaw" baseball league that tried to become a third major league. Federal League owners formed their teams in 1913 and raided the American and National leagues for players. The new league survived for only two seasons.

major leagues—The highest level of organized baseball. After the Federal League collapsed, only teams belonging to the American and National leagues could be called major leagues.

minor leagues—The lower levels of organized baseball. Most players begin their careers in the minors. Only the best players work their way up to the major leagues.

Murderers' Row—The nickname given to the hard-hitting sluggers of the 1927 Yankees. Five of the eight starting players batted over .300 that year.

old-timers' game—An exhibition game played by retired major league stars.

pennant—A team that "wins a pennant" has won its league championship. Pennant winners go on to play in the World Series.

pinch hitter—A player who is put in a game to bat for another player.

reform school—A cross between a prison and a school. Delinquent youths are sent to reform schools in hopes of teaching them to be useful citizens.

rookie—A ballplayer who is playing in the majors for the first time.

scout—Someone who checks out young ballplayers to see if they have what it takes to play professional baseball.

shutout—A game in which a pitcher prevents the opposing team from scoring.

slump—A time during the season when everything seems to go wrong for a ballplayer. Batters who are in a slump cannot get a hit no matter how hard they try.

spring training—The weeks during which teams send their players to warm-weather states to prepare for the upcoming season.

MORE GOOD READING ABOUT BABE RUTH

Creamer, Robert W. *Babe: The Legend Comes to Life.* New York: Simon & Schuster, 1974.

Dickey, Glenn. "A Man Named Ruth" and "Window Breakers," in *The History of American League Baseball Since 1901.* New York: Stein and Day Publishers, 1980.

Fleming, G. H. *Murderers' Row.* New York: William Morrow and Company, 1985.

Gallagher, Mark. *Day by Day in New York Yankees History.* New York: Leisure Press, 1983.

Ruth, Babe (as told to Bob Considine). *The Babe Ruth Story.* New York: E. P. Dutton & Co., 1948.

Smith, Robert. *Babe Ruth's America.* New York: Thomas Crowell Company, 1974.

BABE RUTH TRIVIA QUIZ

1: Hank Aaron hit 755 home runs between 1954 and 1976.

2: Lou Gehrig, the Babe's teammate on the Yankees, holds the record. The Iron Horse hit 23 bases-loaded home runs between 1923 and 1939.

3: The Babe still holds the following records:
Most runs scored in a season (modern record): 177 (1921).
Most total bases in a season: 457 (1921).
Most bases on balls in a season: 170 (1923).
Highest batting average, World Series: .625 (1928).
Most home runs, World Series game: 3 (1928); Reggie Jackson tied the record in 1977.
Winning pitcher, longest World Series game: 14 innings (1916).

4: The Babe could not stand worms or colored butterflies. White butterflies did not upset him, but the sight of an earthworm or a yellow butterfly could send him into a frenzy.

5: The Babe dropped lighted cigar butts inside his teammates' uniform pants while they were getting dressed. The victims often did not know what had happened until their pants legs started to smolder.

6: On hot days the Babe put a wet cabbage leaf under his hat before he took the field.

7: As usual, the Babe was a little vague on names. He shook hands with Waite and said, "Good-bye, Walter."

8: The Babe had what today's players would call "a rifle arm." He threw many runners out at the plate.

9: The Babe often carried a bucket of barbecued ribs with him when he traveled. In the morning the porters had to clean up a berth full of greasy rib bones.

10: The Curtiss Candy Corporation says it named its candy bar for "Baby Ruth" Cleveland. Ruth, the daughter of President Grover Cleveland (1885-1889; 1893-1897), was born in the White House.

Index

All-Star Game 36
American League 23

Baker, Home Run 18
Baltimore, Maryland 9, 14, 16
Baltimore Orioles 10, 13, 14
Bendix, William 43
Black Sox scandal 23, 41
Bodie, Ping 20
Boston Braves 37, 38
Boston Red Sox 14-16, 18, 20, 35
Brooklyn Dodgers 18, 39

Carrigan, Rough 15
Chicago Cubs 5, 6, 36
Chicago White Sox 23
Cobb, Ty 23, 43
Considine, Bob 43
Cooperstown, New York 41

Detroit Tigers 16
Doubleday, Abner 41
Dunn, Jack 10, 11, 13, 14
Durocher, Leo 39

Europe 16

Federal League Team 14
France 39
Frazee, Harry 20

Gehrig, Lou 27, 29, 33, 39
Gibson, Josh 25
Great Depression 35

Harlem River 25
Hollywood, California 43
Hoover, President Herbert 33
Huggins, Miller 20, 27, 28, 33, 35
Huston, Colonel Til 20, 25

Japan, 39
Johnson, Walter 43

Landis, Kenesaw Mountain 23-25
Lazzeri, Tony 29
Life magazine 5

Maris, Roger 29
Matthewson, Christy 43
Matthias, Brother 10, 31
McCarthy, Joe 36
Meusel, Bob 29
Mexico City 40
Mount St. Joseph's College 10

National Baseball Hall of Fame 41, 31
New York, 16, 28, 39
New York Giants 23, 25
New York Yankees 5, 6, 9, 16, 20, 23-25, 27, 29, 30, 35-37

Philadelphia Athletics 14, 18
Pittsburgh Pirates 29
Polo Grounds 20, 25
Pride of the Yankees 39
Providence Grays 16

Robinson, Jackie 5
Root, Charlie 6
Ruppert, Colonel Jacob 20, 25, 35, 36
Ruth, Claire 32, 39
Ruth, George 9
Ruth, Helen Woodford 16, 27, 31, 32
Ruth, Kate 9

St, Mary's Industrial School 9-11
St. Mary's Red Sox 10
Smith, Governor Al 25
Sousa, John Philip 25
Speaker, Tris 18

Terrapins 14

United States 18

Walker, Jimmy 28
Walsh, Christy 32
Washington Senators 25
World Series 5, 6, 18, 23, 25, 29, 31, 32, 35, 36
World War I 16
World War II 40

Yankee Stadium 25, 40

Zachery, Tom 29